T5-BQA-094

Date: 11/8/21

J 636.9766 BAN
Bankston, John,
Caring for my new ferret /

PALM BEACH COUNTY
LIBRARY SYSTEM
3650 SUMMIT BLVD.
WEST PALM BEACH, FL 33406

HOW TO CARE FOR YOUR NEW PET

CARING FOR
MY NEW
FERRET

John Bankston

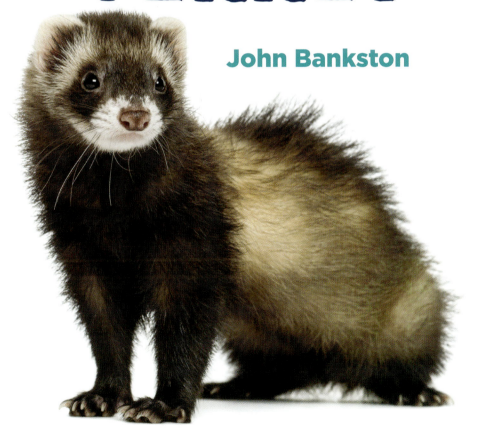

Mitchell Lane

PUBLISHERS

2001 SW 31st Avenue
Hallandale, FL 33009
www.mitchelllane.com

Copyright © 2021 by Mitchell Lane Publishers. All rights reserved. No part of this book may be reproduced without written permission from the publisher. Printed and bound in the United States of America.

First Edition, 2021.

Author: John Bankston
Designer: Ed Morgan
Editor: Morgan Brody

Names/credits:
Title: Caring for My New Ferret / by John Bankston
Description: Hallandale, FL : Mitchell Lane Publishers

Series: How to Care for Your New Pet

Library bound ISBN: 978-1-58415-105-0

eBook ISBN: 978-1-58415-157-9

Photo credits: Freepik.com, Shutterstock

CONTENTS

Words in **bold** throughout can
be found in the Glossary.

Friendly Ferrets

Ferrets have a bad **reputation**. Some places made it against the law to own them. The New York City law calls ferrets "wild, dangerous animals."

Ferret owners disagree. So does the Humane Society. They have helped animals for 140 years. They call ferrets "lively and charming." Dogs bite more often than ferrets.

Ferrets are unlike other pets. They can be litter box trained but are different from cats. Some walk on leashes, but they are not like dogs, either. While ferrets are not for everyone, they can make great pets for the right owner. Before getting a ferret, learn all you can about their **habits**.

DID YOU KNOW?

Ferrets have been pets longer than cats. They were **popular** in Egypt and Italy thousands of years ago.

Ferret Facts

Ferrets are mammals. Mammals are **warm-blooded**. They have live births and raise their young. There are two **species** of ferrets.

The wild black-footed ferret lives in the Great Plains. This part of the United States includes the Dakotas, Nebraska, and Kansas. It was named for the black fur on its feet. Like raccoons, they have a black mask across their eyes.

Wild black-footed ferrets eat **prairie dogs**. These animals disappeared after people moved to the Plains. The wild ferret almost went **extinct**. People saved it by raising baby black-footed ferrets. As adults, they were released into the wild. Thousands now live across the Plains.

DID YOU KNOW?

Baby ferrets are called kittens. Girl ferrets are "jills." Boys are "hobs."

Animals raised as pets or for food are **domesticated**. Domesticated ferrets are related to the weasel, the mink, and the otter. Its closest relative is the European polecat. Domesticated ferrets cannot live in the wild. They need people to take care of them.

Pet ferrets are a little less than two feet long. They weigh two pounds. Their fur is short and brown, black or white. They usually have pink eyes. People once used them for hunting. Today, they often hunt their owner's socks and shoes.

Ferret Proofed

Picture a toddler. Three-year old boys and girls are constantly curious. They put things in their mouth. They escape from backyards or hide in small spaces. Now picture a toddler that slips between the refrigerator and a wall. That's a ferret.

Ferret owners say the tiny animals are incredibly smart. Ferrets use their mouths to escape from cages. They use their head to open unlocked sliding glass doors. They can also push open a shut door. Escaped ferrets are very fast and hard to catch.

Yet you can't keep your ferret in its cage. That will make your ferret very unhappy. There are 24 hours in a day. Ferrets sleep for 20 of them. Then they want to play.

Your ferret will want to stretch its little legs. Ferrets love being around people. Plan on spending at least two hours with your ferret outside of its cage every day.

Before you bring your new pet home, ferret-proof a room. Spare rooms work well. So do living rooms or dining rooms. Kitchens and basements have too many places they can get into trouble. You'll want a room that can be closed off. Have an adult help you cover electrical cords and outlets. Move plants to a higher space. Ferrets love to dig and will scatter dirt all over. They enjoy chewing foam rubber which can make them very sick. Make sure the room is clear of anything they might eat.

If you have other pets, a ferret might not be the right pet. Ferrets think hamsters, gerbils and rabbits are food. Cats and dogs often attack ferrets. *If you have any of these animals, they should never be left alone with your new ferret.*

You will also want to watch younger sisters or brother. Small children sometimes get bit when they play too roughly with ferrets.

Your Ferret's Home

Help your ferret feel at home in your home. Before you get a ferret, set up its home.

Ferrets are **social**. They love being near people. They also like other ferrets. Lots of ferret owners have two. Make sure your ferret home has lots of room.

First, clear space on the floor for a cage that is at least two feet long by two feet wide. Cages are best. **Aquarium**s don't let in enough air and get too hot. Ferrets like to play at night. They might wake you up if the cage is near your bed. Find a place that is cool. They do best at temperatures between 50- and 75-degrees Fahrenheit.

Wire hurts ferret feet. Cover the cage bottom with old towels or sheets. Place a litter box in one corner. Fill it with pellet litter. Do not use clay kitty litter. Dust from clay litter harms their fur. Instead, use pelleted litter. You can also use torn up newspapers. Leave a few inches of space from the top of the box. You will want to change the litter several times a week.

At the other end, put their food bowl. Hang their water bottle from the cage. You will want to make sure they always have lots of fresh water. Ferrets get very thirsty!

Ferrets love to sleep! You can find ferret beds at pet stores. Or use an old shirt or blouse. If you let them sleep on clothing that smells like you, it will help your ferret **bond**.

Ever spend a summer day in a **hammock**? They are great places to nap! Ferrets like hammocks, too. Pet stores sell ferret hammocks. They can be tied to the cage. After setting up the ferret's home, it is time to find your ferret.

DID YOU KNOW?

A group of ferrets is called a "business" or a "busyness."

Finding Your Ferret

Ferrets are sold at pet stores. There are also ferret **breeders**. Breeders know all about the ferret's parents. They can show you how to pick up a ferret. Ferrets need to be at least 10 weeks old before they can go home with you. The breeder should have clean, lively ferrets. The area should also be clean. Good breeders raise healthy ferrets.

Take your time. Get to know your new friend. Picking up a ferret is different from picking up a cat or dog. Find the thick bit of skin on the back of its neck. This is the **scruff**. Grab this, being careful of your nails. Then put your other hand on its bottom. Picking up a ferret by its scruff calms them. This is how mother ferrets carry babies. Ferrets often yawn after being picked up this way.

DID YOU KNOW?

It can be against the law to keep ferrets as pets in New York City, Washington D.C., Hawaii, and California.

You shouldn't be able to feel more than a few ribs. Its eyes should be clear. Its nose shouldn't be runny. Ferrets have a strong smell called **musk**. This is a normal smell.

Ferrets from breeders are usually happy to be held. They might climb into your hair or the hood of your sweatshirt.

The best ferrets are often the ones other people didn't want. Shelters often have ferrets. **Adopting** is a great way to find or give an unwanted ferret a home.

Ferret Training

Young ferrets nip. It's how they play. Ferrets often bite each other. They don't bite very hard. It's just ferret skin is tougher than people skin. They don't mean to hurt you.

Keep new ferrets away from your head. Noses and ears look too much like a fun chew toy. To stop nipping, pick your ferret up by its scruff. Hold its bottom. Do this for a few seconds. If it nips more, pick it up again and make a hissing sound. This is how mom ferrets tell babies "No."

Never shake or hit your ferret. You might hurt it. Remember, it is little and is still learning.

Litter box training is hard. Some ferret owners give up. Make sure there is always a clean litter box. You can try

placing it in the box. If it uses it, reward it with a treat. Be careful. Some ferrets will pretend to go just to get a treat.

The best way to have a well-behaved ferret is lots of playtime. They love playing with socks. They also like cat toys. Don't get toys made from soft rubber or latex. They might swallow bits of it and get sick. *Don't use your hand as a toy.* They will bite it.

Never place a ferret on a table or desk. They don't see very well. It is too easy for them to fall off.

Ferrets also love boxes and tubes. They have even crammed themselves into toilet paper tubes. Find ones they will fit in. Ferrets can also be walked. With a ferret harness and leash, you can keep it safe for walks in the back yard. You might find that playtime with your ferret is your favorite part of the day.

DID YOU KNOW?

A ferret's bite is as strong as a bulldog's.

Ferret Food

Your pet ferret wants to eat the way wild ferrets do. No, it won't go hunting. But it will eat a lot. Ferrets eat eight to ten times a day. Just like cats, they don't overeat. Put food in their bowl and let them nibble all day. If you have two ferrets, make sure they share. Ferrets should have fresh water every day.

And what do ferrets eat? Meat. Because like cats, ferrets are **carnivores**. It's okay to give your ferret kitten food, sometimes. *Do not feed your ferret dog food.* Dog food has too much grain and veggies.

Ferret food lists meat first. That means it has more meat than anything else. Ferrets like lamb and rabbit. Chicken is good, too. Many owners feed them raw food. You don't have to get scraps from the butcher. Instead, buy freeze-dried ferret food. This is frozen food. You add warm water and let it sit. Fifteen minutes later your ferret has a meal with gravy already included.

Cat treats are a good snack. So are cooked eggs. Cooked chicken without any sauce is also nice. Do not give your ferret veggies, fruit, or any sweets. Feeding your ferret right will keep it healthy and happy.

Healthy Ferrets

There is one more thing you must do for your ferret. The week you bring it home, take it to a **veterinarian**. These doctors for animals can help keep your ferret healthy.

Vets spot problems you can't see. The vet also makes sure your ferret gets the shots it needs. You will want to bring it in every year for a check-up.

Spending time with your ferret helps keep it healthy. You will see if something is wrong. If it isn't eating or going to the bathroom, your ferret needs to see the vet. Did you know a ferret can catch the flu? If you or people you know have the flu, you can give it to your ferret. Ferrets with the flu usually get better in a few days—faster than most people.

Ferret is from the Latin word for thief. Pet ferrets love to steal their owners' socks, shirts and even boots!

Ferrets need a lot of love and care. People who have ferrets believe this unusual and fun pet is worth it.

SHOPPING LIST

This is a list of some things your ferret will need:

- ☐ Ferret cage

- ☐ High quality ferret food

- ☐ Ferret treats

- ☐ Bedding

- ☐ Food bowl/water bottle

- ☐ Toys

- ☐ Hammock

- ☐ Litter pan/litter

- ☐ Harness and leash

FIND OUT MORE

Online
There are several sites that will help you raise a healthy and happy ferret:

The Humane Society has information on ferret care and adoption:
https://www.animalhumanesociety.org/adoption/ferret-care

The American Ferret Association has links to ferret shelters in the U.S. and Canada:
http://www.ferret.org/links/shelters.html

Books

Jeffrey, Laura S. *Choosing a Hamster, Gerbil, Guinea pig, Rabbit, Ferret, Mouse, or Rat*. Berkeley Heights, N.J.:Enslow Elementary, 2013.

Klaus, Sandra. *Amazing Facts & Pictures about Ferrets.* CreateSpace: 2016.

Reed, Cristie. *Ferret (You Have a Pet What?!)* Vero Beach: FL: Rourke Educational Media. 2015.

GLOSSARY

adoption
Taking care of someone without a family

aquarium
A glass tank filled with water for turtles or fish

bond
Strong connection, like between a parent and child or a pet and its owner

breeders
People who keep or take care of animals in order to produce similar ones

carnivore
An animal that only eats meat

domesticated
Tame

extinct
No longer existing

habits
Regular behavior

hammock
A hanging bed made from cloth or canvas

musk
Strong smell

popular
Well-liked

prairie dogs
Animal related to the squirrel that lives underground

reputation
Belief about how someone acts

scruff
Loose skin on the back of an animal's neck

social
Happiest in a group

species
A group of similar animals

veterinarian
Doctor who specializes in animal care

warm-blooded
Having blood that always remains warm

BIBLIOGRAPHY

Carver, Marina. "New York ferret fans find foothold as city reconsiders ban." *CNN Wire*. May 28, 2014.

"Ferret Care." The Humane Society. https://www.animalhumanesociety.org/adoption/ferret-care

"How to Train a Ferret." petmd. https://www.petmd.com/ferret/training/evr_ft_ferret_training?page=show

"Is a Ferret the Right Pet For You?" *VetBabble*. January 12, 2019. https://www.vetbabble.com/small-pets/ferrets/is-a-ferret-right-for-you/

Knierim, Ashley. "The Eight Best Ferret Cages of 2019." *The Spruce Pets*. April 24, 2019. https://www.thesprucepets.com/top-ten-ferret-cages-1238669

Kruzer, RVT. Adrienne. "Identifying and Treating Common Ferret Diseases." *The Spruce Pets*. January 12, 2019. https://www.thesprucepets.com/common-ferret-diseases-4145803

McLeod, DVM. Lianne. "Ideas for Toys Your Pet Ferret Might Enjoy." *The Spruce Pets*. January 1, 2019. https://www.thesprucepets.com/toys-for-ferrets-1236791

"Top 10 Reasons Ferrets Make Good Pets." *The Spruce Pets*. February 11, 2019. https://www.thesprucepets.com/reasons-ferrets-make-good-pets-1236788

"Towards a More Natural Ferret Diet: Whole Prey and Raw Foods," *The Spruce Pets*. November 8, 2018. https://www.thesprucepets.com/natural-ferret-diet-1238662

"What Do Ferrets Eat? A Guide to Feeding Your Ferret," petmd. https://www.petmd.com/ferret/nutrition/evr_ft_nutrition_ferret

INDEX

ABOUT THE AUTHOR

John Bankston

The author of over 100 books for young readers, John Bankston lives in Miami Beach, Florida with his rescue dog Astronaut. His favorite thing is to learn something about an animal that changes his mind. Like many people, he thought ferrets bite a lot. Working on this book, he realized how misunderstood the ferret is. He hopes this book will change how others feel about ferrets, too.